LANDSCAPE OF ENVIES

LANDSCAPE OF ENVIES

Jean-Yves Solinga

FIRST EDITION

Little Red Tree Publishing, LLC,
635 Ocean Avenue, New London, CT 06320

Other books by Jean-Yves Solinga:

Clair-Obscur of the Soul (2008)
Clair-Obscur de l'âme (2008)
In the Shade of a Flower (2009)

Copyright © 2010 Jean-Yves Solinga

All rights are reserved under International and Pan-American Copyright Conventions. Except for brief passages quoted in a newspaper, magazine, radio or television review, no part of this book may be reproduced in any form or by any means, electronic or mechanical, including photocopying and recording, or by any information storage and retrieval system, without permission in writing from the publisher. All photographs and paintings in this book are by the kind permission of Jean-Yves Solinga.

First Edition, 2010, manufactured in USA
1 2 3 4 5 6 7 8 9 10

Cover and Book Design:
Michael John Linnard, MCSD

Front cover: *Mont Sainte-Victoire (1882-1885)*, by Paul Cézanne (1839-1906). In the public domain, currently housed in The Courtauld Institute Galleries, London.

Painting on page 54 of Jean-Yves Solinga, titled *At Bartleby's* is by Elaine G Mills.

Library of Congress Cataloging-in-Publication Data

Solinga, Jean-Yves
  Landscape of Envies / Jean-Yves Solinga. -- 1st ed.
    p. cm.
  Includes glossary and index.
  ISBN 978-1-935656-02-9 (pbk. : alk. paper)
1. Poetry. I. Title.

PS3602.R738O15 2010
811'.6--dc22
                        2010013858

Little Red Tree Publishing, LLC
635 Ocean Avenue,
New London, CT 06320
website: www.littleredtree.com

MONT SAINTE-VICTOIRE

There is a path near Marseille.
It lives on a hill facing the Sun
And in the glance of a little boy holding his father's hand.

It is still trying to hide its reddish soil
Among the transparent green of the Maritime Pines.

The landscape defines itself in shades of cascading pastels,
Contrasting vertical surfaces and textures
Of silent granite hills and amorous Cicadas,

The dry coolness of the shade,
The overwhelming presence of the heat
And the sweet acrid scent of the essence of pine needles
Gently oozing their reverence of the World.

Instilling future memories
For the fortunate taking their turn passing through.

Jean-Yves Vincent Solinga
April 2010

"Peculiar moment when spirituality repudiates morality, when happiness is born of the absence of hope, where the mind finds its purpose in the body."

Albert Camus in *Noces: Le Désert*

Le Désert describes Camus' trip to Florence: remembrances of the landscape, paintings, coexistence of beauty and death, last reflections on Man and Happiness.

Comment by Daniel Gerardin [@elliterature.net]

CONTENTS

Foreword by Michael Linnard — xv
Preface — xvii
Introduction by Jean-Yves Solinga — xix

Section I – Outside of the Temple

Outside of the Temple — 2
Of Cats — 5
Arrogance — 6
Man on a Wire — 7
The Magic Field — 9
The End of the World — 13
Of Stardust and Morality — 16
Men in Cages — 19
Elvis in Provence — 20
Grande Illusion — 22
Behind the Curtain — 24
The Souk in Salé — 26
Le souk à Salé [French] — 27
The Danziger Bridge — 28
Gated People — 31
Of Existentialism and DNA — 32
Of Microchips Wafers and Flake of Humanism — 34
Of Macro and Micro Thought — 36
All in a Steamer Trunk — 38
A Beautiful Mind — 39
Dream Sequence 1 — 40
Dream Sequence 2 — 42
Of Beautiful Uniforms and Ugliness — 43
The Pyramid Builder — 45
A Farmer in Kansas — 47
Mesh Mãsh — 48
Scan # 916 — 50

Section II – If Only...

Landscapes	55
Untouchable	56
Intouchable [French]	58
Digitized Happiness	60
A Blindness Of The Soul	62
Years too Late	63
Des années trop tard [French]	64
Waiting for Happiness to Come Back	65
Compassionate Sex	68
Proustian Scene	69
Can't Take It With You	71
Between Literature and Reality	73
Entre la littérature et la réalité [French]	74
Reflection	75
Molecular Memory	77
Death Watch	78
The Fable of the Artist and his Muse	81
Emanations	83
Émanations [French]	85
First Time	87
Little Voices of Guilt and Joy	89
Little by Little	91
Petit à petit [French]	93
A Way With Words	95
Fragile Embrace	97
A Few more Steps	98
No Need to Know	100
If Only...	102
Glossary of Words and Terms	105
Index of Titles and First Lines	109

ACKNOWLEDGEMENTS

I would like to once more thank Michael Linnard of Little Red Tree Publishing for his guidance, support and patience. It is with individuals like Michael and dedicated smaller publishing houses that local talent can find a wider expression, add to the collective expression of lyricism and its continued flourishing.

I would also like to acknowledge the inspirational, emotional support and camaraderie that the poetry scene has given me. New faces who at first were names scribbled on convenient pieces of paper have since become true friends in my life. Albert Camus wrote eloquently and lyrically about the value of this collective solidarity in Mankind.

However, all of this would either be unachievable or less meaningful without the presence of my family and what it represents in the search of a purposeful existence.

Jean-Yves Solinga
Gales Ferry, 2010

FOREWORD

It is without doubt a privilege for Little Red Tree Publishing, of New London, to publish the latest book of poetry from Jean-Yves Solinga called *Landscape of Envies*.

With the publication of *Landscape of Envies*, Jean-Yves has emphatically and unequivocally asserted, in my mind, his right to be called "prolific." And to be more precise, a prolific writer of quality poetry.

As I read Jean-Yves' poetry I am once again thrown into a world of images and concepts. Unlike the "arrow of time," which moves forward and never backward, Jean-Yves' poems move in all directions. Whilst the subject or topic may appear clearly defined, either by the title or the open verses, within a few short words the reader is pushed here and there, over and beyond, below and above, neither unfocussed nor irrelevant: finally leaving you in silence. Like an artist who uses pure color to create exquisite form - with a seemingly endless palette of options - without the slightest suggestion of having worked from life or preparatory sketches and yet it is complete.

Having written the last paragraph before the cover design was finalized, I was truly amazed to find that Jean-Yves had chosen a painting, *Mont Sainte-Victoire*, by Cezanne, to adorn his cover. Aside from the physicality of the painting, which has a very personal meaning and the subject of the poem of the same name, it was by an artist who wanted above all else to define a truth in his own perception of reality. A search for a simplicity and truth that had led Cezanne to redefine perception, in terms other than merely figurative representation, and in so doing laid the path toward total abstraction that others were to follow. In many ways you will find that Jean-Yves is engaged in the same process of fashioning a personal multilayered experience that redefines the world that he and we all live.

In this handsome volume Jean-Yves' has once again created a complete book of poetry, which is both riveting and challenging in its scope as well as penetrating into areas of the human condition that are the refuge and sanctuary of dreamers.

Michael Linnard, CEO
New London, CT 2010

PREFACE

The title *Landscape of Envies* and indeed the source of this book can better be explained by defining "envies" in this work. These 'envies' are not only or solely things and people we want or would like to possess, but also things and people that we would like to change to our liking: for our own altruistic or selfish needs. And so it is akin, often in these poems, to looking over a panorama and wanting something else instead. Something better. More just. Hence theses 'envies'.

I do not like to write as "an exercise in poetry writing." There is nothing wrong with the former and I admire poets who can unfurl topical poems but I would rather not. I am more at ease if the material "presents itself" more naturally.

And so, having finished my latest book of poetry in English, *In The Shade Of A Flower*, I had thought that my ideas would have to be recharged so to speak and I was resigned to take some time to do it. And yet, that book had just been sent to the publisher when a poem ["Landscapes," in this book] came to my mind. Just this noun: without the suffix "of Envies." And the process was renewed. It was not always smooth but the topics came up on their own. Some of my readings in various sources and in particular The Chronicle of Higher Education brought me in contact with issues [some of them old and persistent injustices etc...] that made me add the word "envies," in a slightly more negative tone, to the title of the whole work. I was catching myself frustrated, in my reading and viewing, by some of the inequities that have haunted our kind ever since we had started to express ourselves on the walls of our caves and then gone out to steal someone else's fire and women.

But I must admit that it is so much more rewarding to be inspired by viewing the myriad of movies available and adapting a passage, a look, a returned glance, a remark from a scene. This feeling is the more traditional "envy." The one of capturing, stopping or enjoying what - I will always believe - is still man's superiority over at least today's smartest machines: our very consciousness of Time and Space. And more importantly: "The sound of eyelashes closing upon a kiss."

Gales Ferry, 2010

INTRODUCTION

The proverbial Pandora's Box is fully opened. The era of smarter and faster computer chips and programs is on. I write this in the same tone as Dickens's opening line in *A Christmas Carol*:

"Marley was dead: to begin with. There is no doubt whatever about that... Old Marley was as dead as a door-nail."

Why do I quote this particular passage? Because this seems to be the wisdom and prediction of our times. Computers will progressively learn to do what mankind does and will do it better and faster. But, I contend, the last thing they will learn, if ever, is the *awareness of excitement* of creating something new.

Along this line, I had feared that I would not be able to rekindle that feeling of *the first time* after my first book of poetry. I almost felt envious of that person that I was, then: Hungrily attacking all these different images and feelings. Like finally exploring the other side of the road: Temptation that one's parents had always forbidden. But you knew that it was there all the time. Waiting for you to possess it. At least, you knew, in spite of your frustration, of its existence. Like a lush hanging fruit, all you needed was to wait for Time to make it possible. Time was on your side then.

Hence the personal triumph of the tone of these lines from "Fragile Embrace" where Time itself cannot undo what has been:

The months... the solidity of years of separation

Had been no match against the fluidity of her presence.

***

Could I do it again? How do these artists find in them, or their surroundings, this entrance to new doorways, new experiences? Or are they really new?

Bob Dylan talked about his amazement when considering his relative fluid inspiration for his early work.

Where is that privileged place now? Is it in a completely different genre? Would it be possible to be that person again?

And this is where my reference to machines and Modern Times comes into relevance. Somehow, sitting at my keyboard, frustrated and anguishing about the topic, the need, the value of my poetry, I did indeed find inspiration when I was distracted by something else. The framework of a poem would surprisingly and seemingly come forward in my mind on its own. Or, as was the case in many of these poems, it was the stimulus of the moment, layered with other unrelated memories and a sprinkling of some movie script that acted as the 'binding' ingredient for the narrative.

The thrill was in the *discovery* and in the knowing that there would be other instances as long as I had my wits about me. That as long as I made myself or knew how to make myself *"disponible"* ['available' in the lexicon of André Gide] things and people would open up to me.

It is through this awareness that I find myself superior, in the long run, to any machinery. The latter, I will assume until proven otherwise, is not likely going to experience the same shivers when starting a newly installed program. This concept of human awareness is along the lines of what Blaise Pascal wrote in his Argument concerning *Man and the Universe*: the Universe may destroy Mankind but the glory of Man is in the very consciousness of his own death.

***

If there was an ease, almost an eruption of ideas in

the writing of *Clair-Obscur of the Soul*, I must admit that it was not the case to the same extent for *In the Shade of a Flower* and even less for *Landscape of Envies*. But the effort to distill new visions and revisit old ones produced even more precious moments upon writing them on the screen and reading them out loud.

It was like revisiting the cherished crumbling family farm, seeing the minuscule lake of that first Summer kiss, the chipped library steps where you waited for your friends before going to the movies. The value is in the human glance and its presence: no matter how fragile and ephemeral these are. Just like my poem "Beats of the Universe: a Humanistic View" in which the Galactic beauty exists specifically through very human glance into telescopes.

The first section in this book, "Outside of the Temple," derives its name from a poem with the same title. It deals with my grudging acceptance to accept and analyze the very real and realistic topics that one would find in the headlines: in the dirt of everyday. I find it the responsible thing to do: in the tradition of 'engagement' [political or social commitment] of French writers and philosophers. I find it ironic to apply something as beautiful as lyricism to some of these subjects; but if it magnifies the message, so be it!

This is the message that I received upon my introduction to Victor Hugo's understanding of the duality of mankind: sublime and grotesque. Sometimes at the same time or in succession. And ironically, at times in the same person. The better example of which is Hugo's creation of Quasimodo, a partially made man [Quasi: almost, Modo: fashioned] of *Notre Dame de Paris*. A repulsive man on the outside with a beautiful soul. This explains my instinctive, irrepressible urge to write poems about soldiers and war: how do we deal with the idea, how do we create a situation of sending a plumber from the Bronx with a wife and two children, give him a flame thrower, burn the enemy in a cave and come home to buy a half gallon of milk? Poetry and lyricism cannot and do not have a pass on these issues, hence "The Magic Field."

There is, therefore, in comparison to my previous books, a significant element of 'realism' in this compilation. More death and destruction. More of the complexity and dishonesty of politics. This is due to more solitary time to brood over things. It is not always easy to be delusional enough to overlook the finality of everything and everyone. Sometimes the end is the end.

However, in my opinion, poetry is not a license to be too self-absorbed. I still like a happy medium between the first person romanticism and the universal third. It keeps the ideas from scraping against the extreme walls and destroying their sheen. Nothing can be that important, because, in the final analysis, nothing that we do can change the collective destiny of mankind. But on the individual level: what wonderful things we can do!

This is where I like to explore the space between the quick oxidization of Rimbaud, the exquisite pain of Musset, the bad boy guilt of Baudelaire; and then the moralistic perspective of Pascal and philosophical sharpness of Voltaire. But, nothing equals the combination of the earthy lyricism of Camus and the gentle humanism of Le Clézio. And there is nothing like poetry and writing in general to try to dream or to acquire essences of happiness as the section, entitled "If Only..." implies. And as exemplified in "A Few More Steps," the description of the last breath of intimate feelings can be made beautiful.

***

I have done something that I had rarely done in the past in preparation for a compilation of poems, and that is to quickly and constantly keep notes for new ideas, topics, quotes, for future use. There was an unusual note of immediacy. I didn't like it. I don't like it when the Universe talks to me without being asked. Hence there is at times an even more pronounced bitter sweet quality in some passages such as "The Fable of the Artist and his Muse." But here again, like in the *Fleurs du mal* of Baudelaire, it is the triumph of beauty over anything else that truly, in my mind, defines poetry.

Lastly, I have, as I had done in *In the Shade of a Flower*, sprinkled some French versions of poems.

Jean-Yves solinga
Gales Ferry, January 2010

SECTION I

OUTSIDE OF THE TEMPLE

OUTSIDE OF THE TEMPLE

With the respectful steps of a High Priest,
He walks along the marble columns,
With their greenish striations snaking through the beige stone.

In the Holy of Holies, in the protective clouds of acrid incense,
He can, in spite of her absence, still feel her glance upon him.

Not unlike these moments of youth,
When during more traditional Beatitudes,
He would be overtaken by an eternal peace
Upon looking up at the static white porcelain of the Virgin Mary.

Having become a dead soul since these days,
He had anxiously sought some purity of emotion and spirit,
If not of soul... in some other image.

Standing in front of the golden altar
He can feel the continuing omnipresence
Of her pagan beauty upon him.

He feels emotionally naked within an ambivalence of purity
Found traditionally in the Limbo of infants:

A sort of Purgatory between his need for absolute
Finally met inside this Temple...
... And the dirt of reality outside
With its unsettling noises of things physical and ugly:

The machinery of the everyday.
The grinding of teeth, bodies and souls.
Actions and inactions from inept governments and careless beings.

All this noxious gas seeping and invading from the urban.
Everything coming through the heavy doors.
Through the splits appearing in the weakened wood fiber.

Inside this Temple,
    ... Where he had found solace, love and remembrance.

Away from work schedules, personal ambitions.
Political incompetence and global injustices.
Molecular disintegration and societal inquisitions.

But he could no longer ignore this grinding noise
Akin to the scraping of fingernails on a blackboard.

He had no choice
But to turn away from the altar and face this danger
Thus allocating more of his time from the inner sanctum.

He wistfully thought about his first entrance
In this place of Hope and Remembrance.

Nothing in his fervor had changed since then
Except the urgency imposed by time.

He still held to the beliefs that this edifice represented:

Its sugary artifacts, immortal ceremonies and cottony magic.
The selfishness accorded to the office of High Priest.
The prerogatives of nubile bodies.
The Vestal Virgins silhouetted through translucent silks.
The Chiaroscuros in shades of rich yellow lights
From smoky votive candles.

He had found, like all lovers, a place of purity in an impure world.

But wild eyed virginal happiness
Is meant for the first times of bliss:
Things and people bring in the future
Stuck on the bottom of their shoes

So it came about that he was no longer at ease
In cutting himself off from the solidarity of the streets.

Molecular disintegration and societal imposition were intruding.
They started an infection in the ethics of his morality.

A septicemia that can lead to the death of lyricism
For those completely unconnected
To the catastrophes and collective pain existing at their doors.

Having, in happier times, taken refuge in this house of love
They would hear the cries of political infamy,

The stench of genocides and disease,
Of discrimination of all types of colors and shapes.

An unfiltered wind had come at them
In spite of the screens of lyricism.

These screens would from time to time give way
And their tender lace would allow the dirt of history to reach them.

Turning his back on the altar of Hope and Remembrance
He started to chronicle the impurities of the landscape:

Using syntax and rhythms in fashioning a supernatural mesh
In order to minimize the dirt inside this Temple...

    ... Where he had found so much solace, love and remembrance.

Inspired by the Nineteenth Century's view of the poet as an at times, haughty visionary leader and chronicler of their societies

OF CATS

A sort of unease sets in after three days:
Small apartment and two cats.

Democracy being what it is,
The law of the behavior of the many sets the tone.

Thus it is how, and when, the abnormal, the paranormal
Invade the fabric of the days... and noisy nights.

The Yin takes over the Yang.
The accepted, the sequential, the algebraic and the stable

Are chased out of daily reality, leaving you now
Questioning your human rationality and instincts.

Such inbred niceness as politely looking
Into your interlocutor's eyes:

Instead of basic eye contact
Meeting now with disdainful, beautiful, cold ignorance.

Elementary acknowledgment of one's call
Received with prompt turning of rump and awkward silence.

Seemingly asking for gentle stroke of fur
Rewarded by treacherous hiss and drawn out claws.

A few days of this theatre of the surreal,
Inquisitorial imposition of the "etiquette" of detainee camps,

Leaving one thinking that you are
The only sane inmate in a colony of narcissistic sadists.

Could these animals represent people we know?

ARROGANCE

Ultimate and pitiful. Sterile arrogance.
People living in the sands of dehydrated Africa.

Politicians worried, in their proximity, about imperfections
In the make up of social, religious and sexual minorities.

Forgotten crumbling infrastructures above our heads,
Modern neglect flattening features of old cultures and archeology.

Incapacity to learn
From the immediacy of the very dirt under our feet.

Dubious soul searching instead in dusty religious texts,
Written in hermetic syntax by invisible deities,

In order to find in petrified thoughts,
Solutions to unanticipated future issues.

Statistical evidence of cataclysmic weather changes,
Asteroid impact and eventual frigid end to our Solar System.

And… we hear of distant
Pre-Galilean, pre-Copernicus sightings,

Of mankind's self-serving, self-centered importance
In this Martian feature.

Thoughts on media commentaries of photographs on Martian surface of, apparently, the face of a man.

MAN ON A WIRE

For a while... *They* were united in gentle splendor:
A metallic nuptial link made of youthful bravado.

Self confidence in one's inner ear stability
And indestructible acrobatic talent,

With unblinking conviction in the inevitable reality
That the next seconds will turn into an extended future.

A spidery man on an umbilical cord,
With filaments of Hope and Belief,

Walking on a curve apparently
Running with the natural organic sap of tree vines.

Surrounded with a blend of tall grass of the fertile Savannahs
Made of the cold efficiency of glass and steel.

These towers were briefly united
In a crystal clear wind swept ceremony

With, as audience, a technological ancestor of heights
In the quiet harbor:

Still and untiringly lighting concepts
Such as tolerance and charity.

Along with hushed whispers and stifled anguish.
All these things... all these people as awed witnesses.

These simple lined structures, on that fateful day,
At their symbolic apex of the illusion and delusion of man.

Modern man...thinking, in his engineering head
That nothing and no one would dare cause him or them... harm.

Nothing could be taken away that is defined, at its core,

By such a stately value.

It was a day found
At a cross road. A wedding:

Of a single, slightly demented
And beautiful homage to things and humanity.

A grainy picture remains today of a man
Whose very physical frailty and susceptibility,

Gave to these few moments,
Between these stern towers,

The aura of the innocence of the breathlessness
Of children at the circus.

It all seems now like an unintended prophetic metaphor
For man's everlasting resolve and ambition.

These towers were united,
And will remain so in our minds,

Thanks to the vaporous exploit
Of a single man on a wavy wire...

Precursory image
Worthy of quasi old testament wisdom,

In its visual incongruity,
Of things fragile and ephemeral.

Reflection on Phillippe Petit's August 7, 1974 tightrope exploit between the Twin Towers and the movie by the same name.

THE MAGIC FIELD

It happened on a walk
Through his favorite part of the modest woods
In back of his modest house.

Retired military non-com, going to traditional pasture
In the pungent earth of West Virginia.

The path beyond the break in the fence
Curves into a sort of gentle culvert

And in the Spring flowers,
Outsiders would not think of continuing.

He liked to think that nature... at this point,
Had decided to be left alone.

He would replay
His last remaining years:

Having spent his whole professional life
Surrounded by the living, the dying and the dead.

He takes a left past the old maple.
This tree, untouched by human hands,
Branches too low to the ground,

Had done as it wanted:
Becoming a sort of gate keeper in his eyes.

... A few more steps...
And no more evidence of humanity or society.
The neutrality of Nature. It was just... There.

It acted as a blank screen
Against which he could reflect his own presence... his conscience.

He could feel a discernible pounding on his temples.
An opaque bright light flashed by,

Landscape of Envies

As he felt shoved from the middle of his back
Into the blackness of Things.

The voice of his corpsman yelling invectives at the enemy.
The smell of gun powder mixed with diesel.

Rain drops of mud gently spreading around the fox hole
And this corpsman yelling and crying.

In the mud, a little above them, at the edge of the hole,
A headless body hanging upside down.

He is still trying to decipher the name backward.
It was the newest guy from Boston.
The company philosopher. The college man.

The one who had names
For all the things that were happening to them:
Beautiful ethereal concepts.

He found himself on the grass,
Looking up at blotches of sunlight through the leaves.
Flushed, full of sweat and burning in his eyes.

Back to his house and his worried wife,
Upstairs to the seclusion of his room,

He reached to the left in the back of his closet.
Taking out a black plastic cover and laying it on the bed.

Inside his dress uniform. In full regalia.
With medals still on the breast.

Silver and Gold reflections for things done and seen.
And he starts to cry like a little boy that used to be.

That day... when scolded by his mother,
Having let his brother get the blame:

"What hurts me," she had said, "is that you knew better."

Heard around the faculty dining room table: "The soldier has often been the person who reconciles societies' concepts with reality. Something like a street wise Plato."

A typical deserted passage way in hill top village during the midday heat in Provence.

THE END OF THE WORLD

To the East, the hills that open up on Cannes.
To the South, the valley just before Saint Tropez.

To the North-West, the imprint of Roman ruins.
South-West the beginnings of luscious Rosés wines.

Years and then centuries. Sedentary men and women.
Invading hordes of troops and tourists.

Some armed. Others barely dressed. Some undressed.
Whitish rocky hills. Mini Grand Canyon of Verdon

Reddish coast line and transparent blue inlets.
Mixed with the smell of pine essence.

The gentle hiss through the leaves of olive groves.
The immortal prey birds in the eternally blue sky.

Tortuous paths as quasi roads
Offering religion inspiring hairpin turns.

Confusing indicators
Doing their very best to keep you out and in circles.

At the top of mountain, gravity defying cluster of homes.
Village with public face of grayish walls,
Reflecting an even deeper gray silence.

Anti-tourists winding alleys
Recalling mountain passes of movie lore
Perfect for sneak attack from above.

No signs. And no signs of life.
Pre World War Two sun blanched painted publicity
Of long gone apéritifs.

On this... their third attempt, like faithful Crusaders
At finding the inner Sanctum of this village.

Its purpose for having a name on the map.
A town… seemingly without a purpose. Without a soul.

They walk down an intestine like alley.
Medieval roughness of stones and shy algae showing.

Even the sun has left them to their own compass.
One last right hand turn… one last attempt.

And then… Magic. The magic of some places on Earth.
A precious center of nondescript geometric shape.

Unimpressed by outside Euclidean nomenclature.
Quiet activity of quiet people:

Wealth upon wealth of vegetables for Ratatouille,
Pregnant figs and day old creamy goat cheese.

Aromatic home-made wild-boar sausage
And crimson fleshed cured hams.

Wines from down the hill
And from the population's soul.

Yards of yellow table cloth
Imprinted throughout with designs of lazy olive branches.

Privileged vocabulary rolling off the vendors' tongues:
"Château Neuf du Pape," "Melons de Cavaillon"

The visitors have gone through a cultural worm hole,
To this place where modern society lives in another century.

Shops haphazardly opened and then closed.
Dogs and babies running freely.

They find a timid shop on the left,
Hiding behind an old well.

Yes! The one with the crystalline chimes.

Those made of splintered scales from local multi colored rocks.

The incongruity continues
The owner… impeccably dressed.

Tailored black dress pants.
Starched white shirt with sleeves knowingly folded back.

Impeccable also the mannerism and speech.
A retired Tax Inspector, now artist.
Complete with a refined and peaceful demeanor.

"Why are you here?"
"This, Monsieur," he replies… "is the end of the World"

To Elaine, Robert and Elizabeth, Marc and Nicole in Mons, Provence.

OF STARDUST AND MORALITY

Sparkling intelligence and stellar accomplishments.
Wondrous societies and wonders of cultures.

Impeccable otherworldly crystalline piano compositions.
Mathematical equations with embroidered beauty.

A sparkle, it would seem in any god's eyes
And yet...

Litanies of mindless acts .
Destruction unleashed upon environment and each other,

In the name of convenience.
Inconvenience. Color of uniform or skin.

Local dialect. Belief. Or disbelief:
With often predictable results.

Corrosive chemicals in the land.
In our souls. In our veins.

Seas of plastics bags in the Pacific.
Mediterranean sea of garbage dumps.

Annals of History written in endless persecutions.
Clever tortures in the name of clever institutions.
Found in intricate applications of laws on tablets of fears.

Exalting the names of alternating
Vaporous or fossilized guiding presences.

Unfair societies judged by unjust judges
The list is nauseating and incomplete:

Making one envy the grandiose molecular quiet
Of our mother substance...

... This... the stardust of nuclear beginnings.

How ironic to seemingly find more egalitarian justice
At the elemental chemical, biological level.

To find a harsh beauty in the evenhanded treatment...

... A wisdom in the format of blind universal formulas
In the blindness of physical laws,

... A fibrous beauty
In the gratuitous energy of quasars,

With no particular agenda or creed
Than that of blind obedience to some field theory.

What must we do with this irony?

That there would be more dignity in nothingness
Than the result of reflective intelligence
Coming out of the slime of prehistory?

Let us hope, therefore, that what we are witnessing
In the humane race, at this... its midpoint,

Between the elemental beastly brain
And the ethereal pure thought of the far future,

An awkward teenage stage.
A halfway between dust and perfection.

A galactic crossroad: with minds of enough reflective capacity,
Upon our societal actions and abuses,

To reflect upon the putrid fermenting leftovers
Of our animalistic behavior.

With leftovers of reptilian aggression.
Leftovers of cave dwelling, competition and survival.

That would explain, not pardon,
In this... a cocktail of intelligence, purpose or sadistic pleasure,

The genocides, the rapes and criminality
Of the chronicles of our history pages.

The basic elements of star dust
Cannot take the blame for all this.

Hoping that our instinct for survival,
Added to some pure logic, will filter out

The worst of the vile and pass on the good:
Extracting a milder version of us.

... All this, at a place in Time and Space,
Full of revulsion, making one dare to sadly fantasize

That this... the Third Planet from the Sun

Would have been better served without this last crucial step
Into consciousness... in our Evolution.

Reflection on the obituary by Dennis Overbye : "... Geoffrey Burbidge, an English physicist who became a towering figure in astronomy by helping to explain how people and everything else are made of stardust."

Heard around the dinner table: "Had we not evolved, the African elephants would not have missed us."

MEN IN CAGES

Life, mindlessly multiplying life and demeaning it.
The unfortunate reptilian left over in our brains
Seeing less value in the overwhelmingly plentiful.

Bringing up images of the laws of pure mercantilism:
Graphs of X and Y coordinates
From University Macro-Economics days:

Making the too easily acquired,
The too cheaply available... disdainful, worthy of neglect.

Losing some our humanity by taking
The precious individuality away from others.

The quasi mechanical replicating of Humanity,
Not imposing restraints on our primordial instincts.
Not giving a more collective humanistic face to our replenishing,

Leading to this affront to cosmological luck
Of the probability of generating, on this, the Third planet,
Sun drenched fields of Sunflowers
In the pine scented hills of the Mediterranean.

Like the Canaries in the coal mines,
These men in cages are the pliable but fragile emblematic faces
Of the disregard shown toward our earthly domain.

Heard around a table: "The odds against the formation of something like an Earth environment makes how we treat it that much more obscene."

Reflections on a documentary on the population explosion about men living in iron cages as 'bedrooms' of buildings in congested Hong Hong 2009.

ELVIS IN PROVENCE

Greater than life… he stood there.
Slashes of Chiaroscuros over his pretty face.

Bluish green shadows from the leaves of the plane trees.
The taste of burnt pollen and dry pinède.

Staccato of invisible cicadas from dry creeks.
Dry white heat flowing from washed out granite hills:

Creating an intoxicating imbalance of the soul,
Making you question seemingly incongruous visions.

Imperceptible sway of his hips
At the beat of musical sound from earplugs.

Quick reach, à la Western,
Into tight, immaculate Jeans pocket.

Adept backstroke of the comb
Into glistening black hair.

Virile Cowboy like stance.
Bouncing of the steel ball in his left palm.

Feet firmly inside the tracing of regulation circle.
Last wiggle before letting go the projectile.

Name calling from admirers and detractors
Alcohol from Anisette fueling the air.

Moment of truth for reputation
To be debated endlessly in the cool nights at corner café.

American observer
Savoring the power of symbols.

This would-be Elvis
Playing impeccable *pétanque,*

Under and among
The sun drenched majesty of Provence,

Near the priceless Corinthian style
Of Roman columns at Vaison la romaine.

Multiple centuries, multiple cultures,
Cohabitating in the delusion of this deluded figure:

"In the best of all worlds," he whispered to himself.

Elvis playing pétanque in Vaison la romaine, Provence.

GRANDE ILLUSION

He had met her
Not too far from the Mediterranean Sea,

On a twisting road,
Going up the white hills of Provence.

This new land... this new world... this Eldorado.

She had appeared to him
Dressed in olive green fatigues... A tall wiry GI,

An infantry man,
Coming up from the landings in Nice.

Surrounded with the clouds of smoke
And the precious smell of Camel cigarettes about him.

At the café, a tired, disillusioned underground warrior,
Witness to too many double crosses,

Black market coupon starvation
And the uncivilized results of unraveled society.
A short skinny liaison interpreter with a smattering of English.

The other, the bigger than life symbol of milk fed,
Ever present smile, backslapping symbol
Of the end of oppression and suspicion.

French Maquisard sharing handshake and a can of army ration.
Halting sentences in limited respective vocabulary,

Leading to genuine deep understanding of human solidarity.
Leaving the French soldier enamored with this culture

Seemingly made of a special fiber.
Seeing gentle electricity in this lanky man's blue eyes,

Lighting visions of endless wheat fields
From the middle of this endless continent.

There was a goodness
In the self assured movement of this ex Kansas farmer.

Only kindness could exist
Under such a clean slate in this Brave New World.

But illusions, like Santa Claus,
Are created to simplify the world of children,

While for adults, are left the blemished pages of History.

This is what came to the Frenchman's mind
As he noticed that the "Whites Only" sign
Did not pertain to him as a new Caucasian immigrant:

While Black American soldiers drank down the hall.

Newport News Virginia circa 1950.
French immigrant's first hours in the United States.

BEHIND THE CURTAIN

He stood there, his heart and soul
Full of the vacuum of doubt.

Envious of these people
Descendants of the clan of "certitude."

He… unfortunately, lacked the divinely burnt birth marks,
The manmade dark tattoos, the mutilations of body and mind,

Declaring to the world
His inner structural beauty of Biblical swirls.

His abject agnosticism had kept him
Walking a landscape of manly temptations
Of silent moralistic celestial lights:

Things that made more sense
Under the gratuitous absurd warmth of a friendly beach.

He had wandered close to the opened thick doors
Of the Temple of Truth and Pain, feared by the living.

Sheer stubbornness and unbending passion
Forced him up the steps.

Tired of the fight, he half hoped, but was resigned to accept,
The vision of a clueless clown behind the curtain:

The one of his childhood days at the circus
Floppy hat and white face of the Pierrot

The one whose pathetic bumbling
Made him root for the human race.

Pulling back the surprisingly silky fabric
He was fully braced for the apparition…

Having felt, that life was the focus

Of someone else's joke

He saw, instead, confirmation of his suspicion,
The beautiful, collective answer to his fears,

Upon seeing, his own wide eyed... aimless reflection in a mirror.

Prompted by remarks sometimes leaving out the medical staff upon the survival of a seriously sick child in favor of divine interaction.

Also inspired by the haunting view and status of mankind in The Stranger *and* The Plague *by Albert Camus,*

As well as the beloved circus figure of Pierrot the Clown *and how he represents us.*

THE SOUK IN SALÉ

Much too often, cultures,
Like these monstrous characters of the Japanese stage,

Look upon and scare each other.

We view the Other
As gesticulating and barking marionettes.

Retaining only the easiest and most obvious
Hints of us.

While all we should do,
Is to instead give our senses and bodies

Time... to detect
The shy molecules of the Universe trying to reach us.

After all this time and all this travel,
It is the bitter sweet aroma of thousands of droplets

From thousands of black olives, wrinkled by the sun and salt,
Whose alcohol was escaping through the cooling bamboo lattice,

That still links me to this merchant
Who had his grandson offer me one.

Essence of Proustian olives.

LE SOUK À SALÉ [THE SOUK IN SALÉ]

Trop souvent les cultures,
Comme ces personnages monstrueux des danses japonaises,

Se regardent et se font peur.

Nous nous voyons comme des marionnettes
Gesticulantes et aboyantes.

Ne retenant que les indices
Les plus faciles et évidents de chacun.

Alors qu'il ne suffit
Que de laisser à nos sens et à nos corps

Le temps de déceler
Les molécules timides de l'univers qui essaient de nous toucher.

Après tout ce temps et toute cette distance
C'est l'arôme aigre-doux de milliers de gouttelettes

De milliers d'olives noires ridées par le soleil et le sel
À l'alcool s'échappant à travers le tamis de roseaux

Qui me lient au marchand
Qui m'en fit passer une... par son petit-fils.

Parfum d'olives proustiennes.

THE DANZIGER BRIDGE

"Help the People... Help them!"
But we say:

"They are not us... they are Them!"

Shades of the Other on their skins.
They carry their emotional foreign passports in their pockets.

Wrong side of street.
Wrong side of bridge.
Wrong side of life.

Wrong side of the tracks, countries and continents.
Wrong side of battles and History.

Dusty Alamo. Frozen Moscow. Windy Trafalgar.
Louisiana Purchase. And beads for Manhattan.
The historic lottery of weather or time of day.

Of tired infantry soldiers and dead charging horses.
Of overstated mythology and callous decisions.

Weave a flag... Wave a flag:
Big... So that it will cover any shortcomings.

Time to tabulate:

We'll tell you a tale in schools and books.
Brave and free are we all.

Pastoral scenes of late New England November Pilgrim feast.
Prediluvian friendship. The one before the killings.

Then after fratricidal wars,
Hand full of filibustering politicians
Retarding civil rights.

Bigoted public servants
With personal, hidden carnal biracial appetites.

University Freshmen lecture halls
With contradicting echoes of Political Sciences.

Of Monroe Doctrines and Philippino invasions.
Of Cuban playgrounds for the American Mob.

Of South American... Economic Monopoly play board
Of needless CIA interventions.
And the neglect of needed African ones.

These things are not us... it's Them, don't you know?
Exceptionalism is an inherent goodness in us.

Help the Man... Help him!
They say: he is sick and hungry!

We'll pay others to get dirty.
Meantime, we'll worry about the make up of his soul.

Is he to be feared?
Do we want his kind on our side of the bridge.

Help the Woman... Help her!
Does she carry the stain of disaster?

Is she following the Sheriff's orders?
Or should she be punished?

Voices from the darkness
Of a relentless self help Puritanical past.

Let's take account. Let's write a moralist play.
Let's talk about the possibilities that have always existed.

Take a look at this metaphor... For what could have been,

But did not come to past:

Yes, it could have happened on that day,
Around that table of twelve men and their apostolic teacher.

A world of temporal imperial regional governor,
And the petty jealousies of religious leaders,

Yes... They could have settled their needs and envies
By the time they would have been served sweet dates and tea.

It was not done then. It still is not being done.

Let us, therefore, take a long bitter drink
Of the cup of humility and shame.

Made from the waters
Found off the shores of Lake Pontchartrain

It will cleanse us
Of the self anointment of Exceptionalism.

Cleanse us from the blindness of our moral fragilities:

... That of being human,
Found, that day, on that bridge to Lake Pontchartrain

No particular collective stain...
... Just the realization of our human weakness... will do.

Reflection of coverage from New Orleans after Katrina:
"Police shot and killed at least five people Sunday after gunmen opened fire on a group of contractors traveling across a bridge on their way to make repairs, authorities said." From an AP report.

Also, inspired by Howard Zine's unblinking work.

GATED PEOPLE

Like a last supper... but for just a few select guests.
At dessert... a vintage Sauterne to wash away guilt.

Excesses of money houses and cajoled politicians,
Suppressed into the muck of tinted happiness.

Angst about the impending death
Of microscopic fertilized ovum in mother of three,

Or exploding flesh of confused villagers,
Conveniently separated by bricks of hypocrisy.

Collateral death from attack helicopters
Or legalized dosage from death row physician,

All these details properly differentiated
By the fine print in the footnotes of dusty books.

At holiday meals,
Awash in Dickensian vapors of injustice,

Protected by thick walls of self contentment,
The haves... eat;

While the have-nots
Start scratching the cement of these walls

With kitchen utensils
Rendered useless for their purpose.

Reflections on the concept of and the message behind 'gated living' on Thanksgiving 2009.

OF EXISTENTIALISM AND DNA

What to do:
And why do we do it?

What to think:
And what part of us should we recognize as its basis?

Our Social standing? Our privileges maybe?
Or the eyes of Others upon us... and their expectations of us?

Or should our molecules have been the suspects all along?

Am I... in reality... my blood or my actions?
Are there brakes on my ambitions
Put into action by my inhibitions?

Are there claims and injustices to settle
Hidden in the push toward our judgment?

A gentle imperceptible biological leaning toward
Apparently ambivalent choices.

Are there chains that restrain or pull us
Toward a different bend? Toward an alternate life altering act?

Are there left over echoes of Big Bang Genesis
In the building of our generosity or evil in our souls?

What is, then... the place for free will
In this blood based chemical world in our veins?

Should we remain unimpressed by these findings?
Remain agnostics of any particular predestination of proclivity?

Should we remain full outstanding members
Of the school of self instruction and auto determination?

Either way... there will come a time,
Sitting in that quiet living room of our future,

When we will speculate on past judgments and actions,
And wonder if some or all of them had been tainted
By the taint of old blood in our veins.

Wonder… if giving a scientific name
To something that had always existed,
In the primordial soup of continent hopping by aimless tribes:

Leading to miscegenation
From all sorts of invasions and impositions,

Had made any difference in the balance of things?

Leaving us to decide that knowledge of ourselves
Is better than ignorance
And then… go about Mankind's business.

Inspired by the study Faces of America led by Henry Louis Gates on genealogy and genetic ancestry.

"I may have royal blood!" he said, coming into the office.

OF MICROCHIPS WAFERS AND FLAKES OF HUMANISM

Nothing like a bath in the cross currents of confusion...
... This immersion into Education.

A professorial look over the intellectual domain
To look into the eyes of leaders in today's youth.

Rich, layered waters in this common bath called Education,
The past, present and future... all in one symbolic place:

From the Socratic Method in the cool shadows
Of a solar Greek world

To the ever cold electronic magic
Of a Magic Board.

Still, the confusion exits,
In the ever increasing confused polemic,

Of the impurities in the unwashed pure technology
Flowing into the sacred purity of knowledge.

The dichotomy of mere human, prodding,
Deliberate intellectual ability,

Versus ever increasing memory and speed
Found in electronic chips
Made of filtered sand and nano-technology.

Leading us to confuse...
... To our ever increasing danger,
And humanistic diminution

That the ability to go fast...
... Is... actual... selected understanding.

Jadedly refusing to ask
What is behind, and beyond, the surface

Of the electron fed world that has exploded
Around and inside our youth.

Confusing quick access
To mind numbing democratic internet stupidity

Of demographically multiple
Fifteen minutes of fame... for meaningful introspection.

Making that scene from Fahrenheit 451...
... The opinion of the young house wife...

The terrible and horrifying metaphor
For what passes as relevant knowledge.

Making possible,
In a society of instant search for information,

The answer in a college level class
To an easily acquired important historic question...

... A slew of non sequitur surrealistic responses.

―――――――――――

Having looked behind the curtain, we find
That the Wizard has feet of clay and trickery in his eyes.

Leaving us thinking that more wisdom
Lives outside in that Black and White world...

That practical and tactile world
Of Dorothy's Grandma's chicken coop...

... The one in her previous...
Monochrome... Human... paced life.

Thoughts on secondary education:
Heard every time a life changing innovation enters our society:
"You wait... with this, the youth of tomorrow will have unlimited and total access to in-depth knowledge."
"Le plus ça change... le plus c'est la même chose." French dictum.

OF MACRO AND MICRO THOUGHTS

Truly heartfelt sadness.
One based in absolute conviction.
Conviction and certainty he could have, for once, done without.

The scientifically determined date.
A predicted mortal 'visit'.
An unwanted would be personal watershed in his life.

There would indeed be no easy way out for him.
Organic time would be on the side of decrepitude.

Putting down the Sunday paper
Next to the gentle warmth of his coffee:

"So, I will have known by that date
Either liquefied mineral incineration or cold molecular implosion."

Facing the imaginary apocalyptic Casino table
With odds of collective worldwide mortal and celestial crapshoot.

The bets go in : « Faites vos jeux. Rien ne va plus »:
All the chips on red and none left alone on the green velvet cloth.

Projecting into that future,
He will have, by that date in time,

Had the certain encounter
With either an individual or a collective
Tabulation of things and people.

But there would have existed, either way,
This most exquisite of human reaction:

That is, its contempt for inevitable demise
And its touching attempt to overcome it,

Residing in what would have been
The object of his last thought...
... her.

Thus offering a future reader
The very glorious human satisfaction

Of contradicting the petrified blandness
Characteristic of the unsympathetic Universe

With the very sanguine, visceral, pulsating
Solidarity and empathy...

... Found distilled in that distant reader's... humid glance.

Reflection on article on the Russian scientists' effort to deflect Asteroid 99942 Apophis, named after the Egyptian god of destruction.

ALL IN A STEAMER TRUNK

Somewhere, someone had these remains of them.
Stolen artifacts of transported families.

Identity in these identifying marks
Made of coarse cotton and braided rugs.

Mediterranean colorful tablecloth
Of proud sunflowers and firm olives.

Wedding silver and communion lace
With parents' initials and dessert wine stains.

Tempting goods
Of someone else's life and things

On isolated big city dock
In front of insensitive eyes.

Heirlooms constructed of foreign things
In strange languages and costumes

Filling the pages of family genealogy
Along with snapshots of unknown festivals.

All these pieces of old spaces
And last links to emotional past.

Now dispersed in unknowing hands
And unaware minds

Of these last remnants
Of solid pieces left behind.

Reflections on documentary of Ellis Island and thefts suffered by some families.

A BEAUTIFUL MIND

Scalloped sided black and white picture.
A porch as a setting... any setting. Anywhere in people's lives.

A golden retriever. Smiles in the squinty Summer sun.
An occasion of obscure importance and of unknown purpose.

Faces of momentary immortality and fluidity
Holding slippery toddlers and sweaty drinks.

Trying to link the past to anything tangible in the present.
Trying to make these two dimensional memories

Fit in the rich multidimensional relationship
Of a mother's intermingled existence in her daughter's.

That is when you realize and appreciate
The unequalled beauty... The majesty of the human spirit,

Differentiated from simple, organic, molecular existence,
With no attachment to Things and People in time,

When the bed ridden voice says of her daughter's picture:
"Did she have any children?"

Upon witnessing the increasing loss of memory of a family member.

DREAM SEQUENCE 1

They had done it.
An announcement from the neighborhood Council,

The police
Would turn in their remaining hand guns.

This following an article of rumors
Of doors seen with no locks.

The finance office at City Hall
Having renovated all the schools

And emptied the orphanages
Would turn back allocated money.

The last military base near the capital
Will be an impressive park

Overlooking an ocean inlet
Full of marine life.

The armory will make a splendid
New art and sciences center.

He was reading all this from his home newspaper
As gentle drops were rolling off his forehead.

He fully woke up to the sound
And flying mud of trench warfare,

Drenched in the warm sweat
Of his body's unsuccessful attempt

At cooling off his temperature
From full gangrenous septicemia

From a bullet in his smelly leg

Outside of the Temple

In a world of killing and maiming,

Young men screaming and babies crying.
In a world where mindless collective murder

Had been selectively embraced and properly rewarded
And love and tolerance relegated to a moribund concept.

Dreaming in the fields of World War One.
Veterans Day Eve, 2009.

DREAM SEQUENCE 2

Ripples of fresh water from dark green inner hills
Gently bending the fertile marsh reeds at their base.

Cadenced curves of immaculate grayish white dunes
Filled with the sweet sour sound of stationary sea gulls in the wind.

Ordered sounds of cities breathing in crystalline air
From continental clean lungs of lonely plains.

Abandoned scars of horrible history reclaimed by green vines.
Villages of genocides now re-civilized by wild fauna.

Mankind and animals giving each other living space
In a surprisingly egalitarian mode of existence.

Last minute realization, by one side, that both
Were quickly running out of space, air, water and time.

When a firm tug on his arm startled him:
"It's time for you to guard the food bags."

Waking up in a world of forty billions souls.

OF BEAUTIFUL UNIFORMS AND UGLINESS

A uniform of electric blue,
Blood red stripes along the trousers,
Making any Gendarme appear taller.

Solid color and tapered look of jacket
Giving a fit elegance to the wearer
And gasp of pride to the protected.

His, had been a life saving decision... to join the military:
Catastrophic unemployment and near starvation
Between the Wars and middle of Economic Depression.

Four children to feed and sick elders.
Jealous and distant selfish family.
Alone and hungry among the multitude and plenty.

Hence the proverbial lifeline of steady job.
Just a job. It could have been the sleepy post office.
And surely not the uniform. Though he was so handsome!

And surely not the days on the road.
The brutal, calculating ambitious officers.
The eventual inhuman sadism of some.

He just wanted to eat...

All would have been well...
... For we do learn to sacrifice our comfort for our own.

All would have been bearable...
... For injustices are often part of unjust laws.

All would have been eventually forgotten... forgiven...
... We have to survive... And the survivors can hide the history.

All would have disappeared with time...
... If it had not been the sleepless nights,

The haunting and haunted glances of these families.
The last look upon the last minutes of their freedom
Upon the closing of the cattle railroad cars
To the camps of infamy.

The macrocosm of the hopelessness of humanity
In the microcosm of these individual groups.
That, by their silence, had seemingly lost
The will, the energy to question and rebel.

Yes... the handsome soldier had survived
The physical wounds from the mechanism of this machinery.

Yes... he did get to embrace his family for another day;
But he could never clean the stains off the silky blue wool.

Inspired, among many others, by Claude Miller's film A Secret,
*about the roundup of the Jewish communities during Vichy France
And other infamous roundups of History by otherwise apparently
'enlightened' societies.*

THE PYRAMID BUILDER

He seems to disappear
In the underbrush of the chronicles of History:

Caught inside the binding
That holds the margins of the pages.

Somehow falling out of sight between the folios
That too often run out of space for his name.

We know that he has existed. We see his imprint.
But big books need big pictures
Of oil painted egos in Museums.

Such moments as pre battle rousing inspirational talks
From the rear lines, away from bloody fields,
To bleary eyed soldiers.

Or a monarch's castle found too confining,
A queen's summers apartments too hot:
Resulting in awe inspiring touristy structures.

Another leader's predilection for new or newer wives.
A prime minister bigoted leanings.
A very pious mistress of a king:

Resulting in religious schisms. Countries invaded.
Economic destinies affected.
Tolerance and mercantilism dispersed to the winds.

As one walks through
Stately rooms and turrets of castles
Reflecting on that worker:

The one who laid that ornate oak flooring,
The one who sculpted that marble flower,
Or put the last stone on that pyramid.

The iconic muscles and sweat. Hammer and sickle:

Make for square granite blocks and shafts of wheat.
The height of the pyramid. The bread on the table.

Leaving the tourist wondering:
"Did that worker wish someone would remember him?"

A FARMER IN KANSAS

In his heart where reigned
The clean order of human hierarchies,

He could no longer ignore a spreading fault line
That afternoon, when a knot of guilt overwhelmed him.

It was getting late in his life
And life was redefining itself,

As he held between his fingers
A glass of his special whiskey.

All the time, not being able to reconcile
In his farmer's glance... The one of the animal

Who would end up on our plate
For the pleasure of our palate.

A thought of solidarity for our farmer

MESH MÃSH

He was back in the Medina of that little village,
On the road to the capital. A dusty market place
In the incredible heat of Summer.

On the ground, wooden boxes lined with plastic,
Full of black olives... dripping their inner oils and salts.

Not far: the dark green watermelons with their insides
Of blood red crescents.

The aggravated flies. The placid donkeys.
The acrid smell of the qeśras toasting in the wood ovens.

Things that could make a little boy from the outside
Fear the inside eeriness and distance of the Other.

She came over in her djellãba of sun reflecting white,
Understated vertical light green stripes,
Maternal hint of a smile above the veil.

Her own child eating a tartine of apricot jam.
She gestured, offered one and said: "Mesh Màsh."

No other words were said, understood... or needed,
That day in the African sun.

Back now in glass and steel cocoon,
Sixteen stories above Manhattan,

With evidence of that same fear of the Other
Around the heavy maple table.

He had been trying to reconcile
Unbridgeable diplomatic differences between sides,

As he fondly thought about this concentrated luscious taste
Of apricots on that slice of raspy bread...

That day in his youth.

Thinking it was a perfect example
Of the lasting value of gestures of goodwill
That give perspective in human understanding:

As he absentmindedly doodled on his yellow pad.

Mesh Mãsh transliteration of the Moroccan for apricot
Tartine: slice of bread.
Qesras: bread.
Medina: city center.

SCAN #916

In some future time in our digitized destiny,
In a properly antiseptic clean room

Filled with the unblinking greenish
Cyclopean eyes of microprocessors,

In the restrained buzz from well meaning researchers
Doing what researchers will eventually do…

… Climb on an artificial branch
Outside of the Darwinian forest,

Taking mankind out of the range of the molecular world.
And making it evolve in Things,

Linear, and exponential,
Calculated and calculating,

Grinding its thoughts
Through the gears of predictable equations.

In an industrious age incapable of not wanting
To open any of those post Pandora boxes on the table,

In this world where the gods
Will not survive our selfish demands of them,

Where images from huskers of the idiotic
Will be found in the far flung frontiers of televised competitions,

In our jaded, insatiable need to know
The deepest meaningless secrets of our stars,

In a capitalistic market ready to turn
The most bizarre innovations into teenage games,

In that world of our making…
… A scientist will have perfected that brain scan.

We will know... simply... because we can.

In the true meaning of democratic thought and actions,
The masses will rummage

In the soiled sheets of others
All in the delusional rational that it is a new political right.

———————————

Adultery will no longer carry hidden guilt:
It will be exposed in blotches of chiaroscuro on screens.

Hamlet would not have had to anguish on his own:
The entire kingdom would have known.

Surprise parties
Will be publicized before their inception.

Feelings on first night
Will be crushed as the date comes down the stairs.

Moral squads will rebuke
Some of the on-lookers on side walk bistros

For their prurient thoughts
Provoked by passing short skirts.

Office workers will learn
To dull and scatter

Their hatred of their boss
By taking appropriate amounts of chemicals.

———————————

And somewhere... Somehow...
Groups of recalcitrant

Will run into the woods
And chance dying of treatable cancerous growths

For the joy and privilege of living
In the contented, uninformed awareness

Of what they and their neighbors
Reciprocally think of each other.

Inspired by media reports [2009] of the fledging capacity by scientists of reading brain scans that give very rudimentary evidence of what is being 'seen' or 'felt.'

Shades of Fahrenheit 451.

SECTION II

IF ONLY...

Painting of the author sitting at Bartleby's Café, in Mystic, CT., by Elaine G Mills.

LANDSCAPES

All these hours, all this coffee... in his favorite space
Turned into a place of emotional strain and analysis.

A literary purgatory to expiate his deeds.
Misdeeds, fantasies and lies.

All this time and all this induced anguish
Transformed into blinking photons on bluish screen.

Painting the walls of the future with convoluted passion.
Then... like graffiti, exhibiting them at reading venues,

Crowded with disrespectful espresso machines
And the whine of signals from portable phones.

Poems created
In the fertile silence of his creative cocoon

Experiencing the confused silence
Of still birth from ambivalent public.

Still, the seemingly attainable
And unexplainable drive remained

Of reconstructing pieces of the present
With leftovers of his past.

Holding to the irrational hope that a chance glance
By a first year English teacher

And purchase of his fragile cellulose collection
In a dusty used book stand

Would lead her that night in that distant time
And warm New England winter bed

To let out a teary sigh from her humid heart
As she roams in the now appropriated

And recognizable poetic landscapes of his pages.

UNTOUCHABLE

It is there that she exists. There where Muses' lives end:
Away from the carnal and ordinary of daily life.

There, where the forbidden space
Between the embrace and the need

Will give her the aura of the Madonnas
Found under the transepts of churches.

Made of this beautiful pink marble
Of the burning hills of the Mediterranean,

She had known till then
Only inert mineral warmth.

Stone...
Fashioned in the fever of the moment,

Stone...
Made malleable by the heat of the sculptor's fervor,

She represents now
The plasticity of the hidden desire under the cotton of pleasure.

Her veiled curves were cut
Into the hard marble of the temporal,

Precisely where it offered itself to the intimacy of the chisel
And... once the dust settled on the studio's floor,

Once the discreet sheet having fallen to her feet,
Once the workplace dark and empty,

The artist finds himself immobile and immobilized
In front of his creation...
... A vision of the degree of warm happiness.

Gone, now, a long time ago, into the chaos of reality:

Searching, nevertheless, for a way to reclaim in his arms

The woman hiding behind the object...

... The artist, now in his bed, eyes wide opened,
Tortured by dreams made of mineral clouds.

Between the Artist and his Muse.

INTOUCHABLE [UNTOUCHABLE]

Elle existe là, où les muses finissent leur vie:
A l'abri du prosaïque charnel de tous les jours.

Là, où l'espace défendu entre l'étreinte et le besoin
Lui donnera l'aura des Madones sous les transepts d'églises.

Faite de ce beau marbre rose
Des collines brûlantes méditerranéennes,

Elle n'avait connu jusqu'alors
Qu'une chaleur inerte minérale.

Pierre...
Façonnée dans la fièvre du moment,

Pierre...
Rendue malléable par la chaleur de la ferveur du sculpteur,

Elle représente maintenant
La plasticité du désir caché sous le coton du plaisir.

Ses courbes voilées furent découpées
Dans le marbre dur du temporel,

Justement là où il s'est offert intimement au burin.
Et... une fois la poussière de l'atelier posée au sol,

Une fois le drap protecteur pudique tombé à ses pieds,
Une fois l'atelier noir et vide,

L'artiste se trouve immobile et immobilisé
Devant sa création... vision de la tiédeur d'un bonheur

Disparu il y a longtemps dans le chaos de la réalité :
Cherchant, malgré tout, à recouvrir dans ses bras

La femme qui se cache derrière l'objet...

… Cet artiste, maintenant dans son lit, les yeux ouverts,
Torturé par des fantasmes pierreux.

Entre l'artiste et sa muse.

DIGITIZED HAPPINESS

Running on empty… in empty street.
Coffee fumes as companionship.

Emotional hunger prompts the shuffling
Of past images in his mind.

Spontaneous deep sighs cadenced
With the sharp echoes of heels on sidewalk.

Drops of hope now scattered on the cement
By humid clouds of doubts of the heart.

Static of communication. Silence.
No hearing.

There is nothing on the other side of that solitary reflection
On the empty storefront. And nothing within his confused reach.

The modern man is disconnected.
The plug has been pulled.

This contemporary Titan
Searching for the warm comfort of absent Mother Earth.

Nothing has changed since the Mythological beginnings.
Nothing can be changed in the biology of Things.

The reality is… the wire has been cut.
That part of the world… gone.

The Human. The Humanity
Is still starving for the immediacy of touch.

Flesh craving…
… Craving flesh.

The gaping hole filled instead
With the detritus of binary codes,

If Only...

Giving man a digital closeness
Of shiny copper conductivity.

Coaxial intimacy
Of make belief embrace... in high definition.

All the artifice of the artificial...
... near at hand.

Except, except for that hint of his reflection
On the curve of her precious pupil.

Except for the distinctive perfumed floral essence
Emanating from her overheated flesh.

Looking for Human Warmth in a Modern Technological World.

A BLINDNESS OF THE SOUL

She had prided herself in self-awareness.
She knew where she, things and people had stood.

Woman of the world,
At ease with red wines and hors d'oeuvre.

Fluent in Geo and Real Politicks.
Mistress of retort, repartee and double entendre.

Amusing to hear, pleasant to both sexes.
Fun to have around.

Quick to discern sleepy eyelids in hostess.
Adept at catching sneaky glance of watch from host.

Chameleon of popular politics and mores.
Trend setting of styles of camouflage of unorthodox thoughts.

Flexible of schedule.
Always present and available in order to please.

All these things
In the eyes of others toward her.

All these acquired societal talents
Of apparent sensibilities and sensitivities.

All well-guarded and arranged
Along with her assortment of silk scarves and translucent blouses,

Not far from photographs of Renaissance arcades
Showing couple smiling into setting sun,

Except,
For the distant repressed awareness,

Of the precious value
Of the glances at the heart of that moment,

That had stopped loving each other such a long time ago.

YEARS TOO LATE

Only biblical analogies came to his mind.
Concepts of religious calendars and space.

Times and places of happy endings
In ultimate resurrections of various forms.

Expurgatory ceremonies of any and all sins
With accompanying accoutrements of scented oils,

Burnt offerings in incense holders
And appropriate tears of regrets.

Instead... his soul rooted in the sterility
Of an inexistent ex machina redemption.

Schisms of time of blissful earlier innocence
And guilt stricken post carnal knowledge.

Divine intervention, only part of quaint echoes
Of wide eyed youthful catechism under stained glass windows.

Left now, with clear cut delineations and definitions
In the style of Neo Classical clarity of Clair Obscures

Painted on the emotional canvas of his heart:
Good and Bad nonchalantly facing each other,

As he sits... demoralized, in his leather chair:
The epitome of the self-defining existentialist,

Having proven beyond any personal doubt
The validity of his philosophy.

Whispering to himself:
"If I had died in middle age... I would have died a perfect man."

Reflections of the movie Meet Joe Black.

DES ANNÉES TROP TARD

Rien que des analogies bibliques lui venaient à l'esprit.
Concepts calqués sur les espaces et les calendriers religieux.

Des moments et des sites remplis de belles conclusions
Aux résurrections ultimes et variées.

Cérémonies expurgatoires de tous et de n'importe quels péchés.
Avec accompagnements et accoutrements d'huiles parfumées.

Fumées d'offrandes venues d'encensoirs
Et de larmes de remords convenablement appropriés.

Pendant que... son âme, elle, reste enracinée dans la stérilité
D'une rédemption inexistante ex machina.

Schismes matériels d'une précédente innocence béate.
Celle-ci suivie de la culpabilité de la connaissance charnelle.

Intervention divine, à présent réduite à des échos vieillots
D'un catéchisme à bouche bée sous les vitraux de l'enfance.

Seul... maintenant, face à des délinéations et définitions
Au style néo-classique baigné de clairs-obscurs.

Le tout peint sur le canevas émotionnel d'un cœur
Où le bien et le mal s'observent nonchalamment.

Maintenant assis... démoralisé sur son fauteuil de cuir :
L'existentialiste incarné.

Ayant prouvé hors de tout doute personnel
La validité de sa philosophie.

Alors qu'il se répète :
« Si j'étais mort plus jeune... je serais mort un bon être. »

Réflexions sur le film Meet Joe Black.

WAITING FOR HAPPINESS TO COME BACK

Time and people had divided themselves.
Clocks in lonely kitchens had stopped.

Branches in scary forests had split and broken off.
What had been... could never be again,

And handfuls of diamonds
Turned into their maternal coal.

The renewal of the spectacle
Of everyone's personal Crucifixion was on.

Nails of guilt and sorrow
Would be inserted in extremities,

And at the end of breath and life,
One would know the moment

When distant whimpers... From precious lips,

Would not be able to save
The last morsels of Happiness in the soul.

We would forever be damned to know...
... To know that happiness was behind us,

And would not be able to turn around.

We would walk into the land of darkness and void
And reflect on what it is to feel

That you had no claim on the past
And no more interest in the future.

Like an inconceivable cosmological collision
Two conceptual universes had a contact point:

One where an unavoidable right step forward

Would take us into everlasting void.

While, with our hesitating left foot,
We would still be touching the land of plenty.

We would be able to feel
The residual heat from elemental nothingness

That would have evolved...
... Transformed, exploded... into Everything.

Time would then feel as though it had stopped.
But would not have.

On the other side of this escaping residual warmth,
We would be able to distinguish the eternal cold

Of what it is to live
With the infertility of time in our veins.

Nothing good or bad would ever be.

The scales to measure awareness
Would have been abandoned in the dust: For lack of interest.

It would be a surrealistic world
Of Early Greek Olympian gods

Wasting their hours in caves
In a blackness induced ennui.

It seemed They all had been waiting for Godot...
... Already. All these years ago.

Nobody had told us.
We had not right to know.

These two worlds had pre existed us.
They were inevitably waiting for us.

If Only...

No sense in worrying about them:
Each individual reaches that point only once
... And never again.

Reflections at the intersection of Dante's Divine Comedy *and Becket's* Waiting for Godot.

COMPASSIONATE SEX

He had thought that she had come over for him.
She had not... Just a place to stay.

He had thought that she still loved him.
She did not: she had already met her future husband.

He had never stopped thinking about her. Kept all the letters.
She had to get his address from a mutual friend.

He had thought that he still had a special place in her heart;
All she needed was a place to keep her dog.

He had thought that meeting his mother meant something.
It had not: She just loved good food.

He had thought that being polite
Would mean offering her a social drink.

But... She must have picked up on all of this
And did the humane thing:

Offered him the best sex that she could.

Years later he would awkwardly
Still see compassion in that gesture.

Reflections on the movie by Laura Mana: Sexo por compassion.

PROUSTIAN SCENE

There had always been
A certain restraint in his friend's demeanor,

While for himself, he had had no problems
Expressing personal affection.

Thus he detected
A degree of resistance, a separation from him,

Toward what... between men...
Should have passed as simple expressions of friendship.

Such reaffirming things as a warm extended handshake,
A congratulatory arm around the neck.

"There are types that are more discreet than others,"
He thought to himself.

It was upon hearing of his suicide
That he revisited the pieces of their relationship.

That is when he learned
Of his friend's struggle to reconcile his homosexuality.
Of his anguish under the old standards of behavior.

Of the built-in contradictions and perceived dangers
In the different levels of friendships
And their physical expressions.

The confusing hypocrisies
Of accepted virile intimacy of male team members
That would have been denied to him.

And thus, going over the landscape:
Going over the years of friendship with this man,

Looking for indications:
Of anguish. Envy. Need. Happiness. Sadness...

Or despair...

All the ingredients that fill the hungry voids of anyone's soul,

He discovered how incredibly simple
It should have been to have given his friend
The chance to talk, to verbalize openly.

He was left instead with an image
Of extreme discretion and shyness.
A sophistication of the mind. A gentleness of expression.

Sitting in their favorite coffee shop,
He remembered the way he had brushed aside
Some bred crumbs off the table cloth.

The quasi artistic elegance
In the mundane of mundane gestures
That he had always so much envied in him.

What did it personally say about him?

He remembered being mesmerized
By that scene taking place across the table cloth.

It was upon looking back up
That he literally sensed his friend's glance upon him.

He felt a burning sensation on his cheek
As though he had been caught in an act of voyeurism.

Had he been intruding?
Or had he, for the only time
Been given the privilege of entering this man's soul?

Now by himself, at this same table,
Having taken a sip of coffee,
Looking in awe at a galaxy of bread crumbs.

Inspired by Marcel Proust's characters and Christopher Isherwood's "A Single Man."

Also this comment around this topic: "He was like a snowflake going through life."

CAN'T TAKE IT WITH YOU

Wise words,
From more quiet worlds...
Came to his mind.

No longer the spaces
Of immediate gratification and amoral guidance.

No longer the illusions of delusions
From other spaces and other times.

We learn to adapt
To the more confined alcoves imposed by life.

Living now in the reality
Of slowing electrons and aging molecules

That know only one direction:
Away from us... and away from now.

In the airport,
The elegance of the black leather bag said everything:
Class. Evolution. And good bye.

Immediate and intimate knowledge
Would become impractical and needless.

The truth of all these things
Made the rest necessary and acceptable;

But for one thing...
... It seemed most of his organs

Had decided to leave him behind
And follow her onto that plane.

It was the same movement of the soul
Of years ago in that other airport.

There was nothing he could do then:
There was nothing left... this time.

Just a human form disappearing
Behind uniforms, steel and glass.

The full regalia of apparatus and people
That would efficiently, coldly take her away from him.

He could only think of how much he wanted to be
The pliable leather of her black bag next her warmth:

Murmuring to himself:
"Sometimes a cliché... IS reality."

To the sound of "Every time you go away... [you take a piece of me with you.]"
By Paul Young

BETWEEN LITERATURE AND REALITY

He had heard about her.
He knew everything and nothing.

He had filled in the sketches... the voids of her face
With the smallest crumbs of rumors,

With references to cinema,
With similarities in his past,

With literary resemblances,
With the mannerisms of historic characters.

He was diligently putting away some files
When she came in the office.

Upon turning around he momentarily thought
About one of these glorious moments

When... from his readings... the oxygen of a room
Seems to be lacking as he was gasping for air.

She was the spectacular union
Of fiction and flesh.

He understood by the end of the meeting
That he... was not.

ENTRE LA LITTÉRATURE ET LA RÉALITÉ
[BETWEEN LITERATURE AND REALITY]

Il avait entendu parler d'elle.
Il en savait tout et rien.

Il avait rempli le schéma... les vides de son visage
Des moindres miettes de rumeurs,

De références cinématographiques,
De similarités dans son passé,

De ressemblances littéraires,
De maniérismes de personnages historiques.

Il arrangeait assidûment ses dossiers
Quant elle entra dans le bureau.

En se retournant il pensa momentanément
Connaître un des ces moments glorieux

Où... il avait lu... l'oxygène d'une pièce semble manquer,
L'effort nécessaire pour respirer étant tel.

Elle était l'union spectaculaire
De la fiction et de la chair.

Il comprit, à la fin de l'entretien,
Que lui... ne l'était pas.

REFLECTION

She was at the limit of perfection
Found in sketches, in drawings.

That place of the instantaneous glance of the artist.
The slashing pencil movement on paper, showing no pity.

Trying to stop the Essence of the Thing,
By reducing it to its untouchable fluidity.

Taking it out of the too solid and opaque temporal.
The very same, fatal enemy of the invisibility of the transparent.

She was there... complete and perfect in her vitreous absence:
And yet within reach of his adventurous fingers.

He could, at his leisure,
Draw over the curvature of her lips.

With his index, follow her short cropped hair:
Thus creating a steamy foggy outline.

He could possess her without the least intimacy :
Barely brushing, as he wished, her eye lashes without any bother.

He could approach this geometric purity... enter it,
Without leaving the least organic evidence of his presence.

Like these Mythologies
Where the young man observes his mistress at her bath:

Hidden by the decency of the bushes
Surrounding the necessarily virginal vision.

Now seating at a coffee house table: on this side of life,
Full of cups with blackened residues,

Ill at ease in the midst of strident feminine voices,

Non intelligible conversations from the other table,

He realized that he was filling in
The reddish urbane voids, behind the illusion of this woman,

With the overlaps of his fantasies of unapproachable Beauty
That his mind had ever been able to conceive.

"The absence of things, for Mallarmé, is in a way their own definition, their very best definition. ... It is therefore this absence of beauty at the expressed level that defines beauty itself."

Comment on Mallarmé by E. Noulet quoted in: http://www.unice.fr/AGRÉGATION/dentelle.html

And from the same source a comment by Verhaeren on Mallarmé:

"I have often thought while reading Pages, *about these mirrors placed one facing the other that at the end of their clarity finally reflect, it is true, the same image; but how differently, each in their transparent chambers. Such is the case in the depths of Mallarmé's sentences. Each reflects the given, the idea or feeling of the whole, but differently, concentrating it, as though sucking it, toward the next focal point."*

Observations upon the reflection of a woman's face on the window of a coffee house with, as background, the mercury lit street beyond.

MOLECULAR MEMORY

His steps seemed to remember...
The uneven surface of the cement walk.

The proximity of that heavy wooden dormitory door.
The earthy smell of the ivy covered walls.

The regal oak tree doing its very best to keep,
In relief on its trunk, its own remembrance of lovers.

Multi sensory souvenirs of green lettering
On the metallic presence of street cars:

All witnesses to the microcosm of personal drama
With first row seats to first act and last scene.

Secretive embraces and humid departures
Under emblematic iron lace work.

But to his astonishment,
As he tried to swallow a knot in his throat...

He felt that despite the seemingly
Dense, eternal solidity of Things,

... To his astonishment... He realized that his flesh
Could not remember a time...

Of her... ever not being magically present
In the fibers of his heart.

A sentimental walk by 'that' University building of Undergraduate days.

DEATH WATCH

He could not reconcile the mournful ambiance
With his giddiness at seeing her again.

The contradiction of the very physicality of death
Which these viewings forced upon his jaded attitude.

The antithesis in the stillness of the presence
From the former flamboyant energy of his friend.

All this theater, meant to elicit, to any decent witness,
An ultimate emotional connection

Of what had been, in the darkest confine of jealousy,
His most personal secret nemesis.

And thus, after giving the eulogy...

... After long attempts to untie the lumps in his throat,
While his tie stayed on,

... He had to sit next to his friend's wife.
Next to this woman who should have been his.

Invading, for lack of space between the chairs,
The imaginary line on his right side.

He thus could feel the intimacy
Of her body through the silk of her suit...

... This unapproachable, untouchable woman,
According to society's mores...

He was absentmindedly observing
The metaphor... the source of his morality:

The overlay of the star of David on the coffin
Which did not manage to impose culpability in his heart.

If Only...

After years of long distance infatuation for his friend's wife
He could match his breathing to hers.

All the while concentrating on her slightest body motion,
Trying to separate in his unrestrained fancy

What could have been purely shifts in her posture
From any possible instinctive search for human warmth.

Mas [farm house] in sunflower field, near Aix-en-Provence.

THE FABLE OF THE ARTIST AND HIS MUSE

He had lived in the land of plenty...
... Friends loved the sprint of his humor.

It would jump from misty imagery to the concrete:
From subtle sensuality to the urban silt.

Ideas as transparent as the finest black lingerie
To the blackest of political pronouncements.

Women caused him no fear
As he would approach with the greatest of ease

The ingots of sparkling treasures in the details
Found in the 'quasi-foreplay-value' of the Genesis of friendship.

Colleagues and acquaintances looked forward to his arrival
At frivolous parties and family gatherings

Knowing that he would insert himself
At different levels into different levels of conversation.

But like many great souls he was made
Of complex, brittle... complicated machinery.

Like a beautiful time piece
His... was a mind that was made to accommodate

Only one eventual sister soul... his Muse...
Made, by the magic of chance, to his specifications.

He could only drink... he could only transcribe
Things and visions emanating from this vaporous being
Who appears, so believingly, in our childhood fairy tales.

And so he began the rest of his life:
Alone for the first and last time,

With a far away look in his eyes.
His hands on his chest looking at the lake where they had met.

Remains of streaks of spiritual tears
Still shimmering in blotches in the decreasing sunlight.

Everyday… henceforth… he would dress himself and his mind
For her inevitable reappearance,

While limpid water of other presences
Was trickling within his easy reach.

But having tasted the spectacular molecules
Of the vitality of creative life
He had lost his taste for the template of the mundane.

He was victim to the hidden mortal danger of the artist…
… That of coming across a spectacular Muse
With intricate, complicated sides.

Rich in topography and angles
Made of exact and exacting formulas:
Akin to the ones of Medieval alchemy.

All these details of her that magically, perfectly
Matched the gapping cavity in his heart:

Miraculous geometric volumes,
Worthy of the science of Merlin,

That had, on a fateful day,
Found its perfect and perfected niche
In his soul and body.
Nothing and no one else could or would ever do.

And so, he was dying… in full regalia,
With his crimson vest neatly buttoned to hide to the world
The place where she had lived.

Inspired by the relationship between George Sand and Alfred de Musset.

EMANATIONS

Perfumes with brands of sophisticated Parisian avenues,
Names found on blue signs and white lettering.

Labels mentioning complex mixtures
From knowledgeable technicians...

Professionals
With quasi medieval secrets.

The product coming out of urban laboratories
With walls of stainless steel and cold glass patina.

Sensual, intellectual,
Well researched advertizing.

Emanations
Which he seemingly had always well known :

His mother... In front of the dressing table mirror
Before her evenings out.

The small crystal vial... the one in back of the others,
The one with the pump...

And the result... A cloud... as much present as it was invisible.
An intoxication... Woman was that.

Later on, during interminable receptions,
He would swallow petits fours

Along with gulps of flowery smells
Evaporating from ivory skins

With muscles defined by tennis:
Woman had thus become.

Until the day when this woman
With her flesh full of the curves of the sun

With her skin... mixture of primordial soil,
Multicolored skirt and shining hair,

Fixated him by a simplicity full of the essences of nature
Coming of envies from the other side of his life.

This woman emanated extractions of another world
Opening his soul to the richness of the elemental in things.

Holding his breath...
... Keeping within him molecules of her being in his lungs

The way he used to... as a little boy,
When he would return to his grand parents' farm.

Inspired by La chevelure *de Charles Baudelaire.*

Location: Next to the appetizer table at a diplomatic reception.

ÉMANATIONS

Parfums aux noms sophistiqués d'avenues parisiennes
Trouvés sur des plaques bleues aux lettres blanches.

Étiquetage mentionnant les mélanges savants
Des savants parfumeurs... Secrets professionnels quasi médiévaux

Sortis de l'alchimie des laboratoires urbains
À la patine en inox et verre froids.

Publicités sensuelles,
Intellectuelles et recherchées.

Émanations
Qu'il connaissait personnellement depuis toujours :

Sa mère... Devant le miroir de la grande armoire
Avant les sorties en ville.

La petite fiole en cristal... derrière les autres,
Celle avec la pompe...

Et le résultat...Un nuage... d'autant plus présent qu'invisible.
Une intoxication... la femme c'était ça.

Plus tard, pendant d'interminables soirées,
Il avalait les petits fours

Avec des bouffées de floraisons
S'évaporant de peaux en ivoire

Aux muscles définis par le tennis :
La femme était devenue cela.

Jusqu'au jour où cette femme
A la chair contenant la rondeur du soleil

Au teint mélangé à la terre primordiale,

Jupe multicolore et cheveux luisants,

Le figea de sa simplicité des senteurs terrestres
Provenant des envies de l'autre côté de sa vie.

Cette femme émanait des extractions d'un autre monde
Lui ouvrant l'âme sur les richesses des choses élémentaires.

Retenant sa respiration
Gardant les molécules de cet être dans les poumons.

Comme il le faisait... petit garçon,
Quand il retournait à la ferme de ses grands parents.

Inspiré de La chevelure *de Charles Baudelaire.*

Près de la table des hors d'œuvre à une réception diplomatique.

FIRST TIME

Icons of contradictions whirled in their minds:
The natural timeless beauty.

The inherently physicality of consummation.
And the spirituality of its meaning. To him. To her.

Magically, none of it was lost
In the non-verbal intimacy of the moment.

Everything well impregnated in the whispers of their lips.
The shadows and creases of the jealous curtains.

Witnesses all. The strewn clothing.
The sweaty sheets... and nothing and no one else.

They had in them the individuality
To repel instinctive reaction: Procreation. Instant
gratification.

On his part, it was an impure rich mixture
Of the magnanimous. The patriarchal.

The chauvinism and haughtiness of masculine power,
To singularly deny his claim to eternity. Immortality.

A jaded and emotionally satiated being
Looking into the beautiful amazement of her glance

That he would cherish for the rest of his life...

... He stopped.

An imperceptible smile came to her lips
And a fraternal kiss on the cheek followed.

Her thighs remained opened and her heart pounded
And an act of purely functional importance

Would live as perfumed essence in their separated souls
Long after the flesh had cooled to the chill of the mundane.

Reflections on the movie An Education [2009] *and the scene of non consummation of their first relationship.*

Also, Alfred de Musset's [Lorenzaccio, Rolla] *description of the attraction and repulsion of sensuality.*

LITTLE VOICES OF GUILT AND JOY

They were prisoners of their choices.
True captives of their Existentialist freedom.

Their actions and decisions to be reimbursed
By demands on the integrity of their agnostic souls:
The debt to be theirs alone.

That was the pact that they had emotionally signed
In their late hours coffeehouse whispers:

Committed... bodies and souls
To attractive philosophical concepts
Written on University blackboard swirls.

No authority to sanction their next move.
No green light from above or below.

Nature had done its duty and given them passion
Through reciprocal quivering fingertips over the table.

They could not help but have an envious thought
For these tranquil minds... members of various theologies.

They had both discarded the luxury of transference:
Of guilt, choice and direction.

Left, now in nuptial darkness to their own ethical devices,
As precious pieces of the carnal Universe
Were parting in front of their eyes:

And no one and nothing to absolve them.

The ritual was old...
... But it is always new for the first time... for all.

Alone and left with only their lubricity for covers
Under the harsh lights of full consciousness,

Showing the silhouettes of their intermingled limbs
On the walls... Of a future full of nudity... physical and moral.

With undulating sheets of translucent love and fervor
To counteract the weightiness of the act:

And no one and nothing to blame.

The Chronicle Review, *Section B, March 12, 2010. Article by Michael Ruse 'What Darwin's doubters get wrong':*
"As the Victorians used to say about sexual intercourse, if God decided that we should reproduce in such a disgusting way, then it is for us to accept this fact and put it in context."

"University student couple putting their beliefs to the test."

LITTLE BY LITTLE

There always had been something unreal in the details:
The moments seemed often too much outside of the possible.

The laws of the Universe and happiness
Joyfully bypassed, transgressed:

The glance too eternal.
The skin too silky.

An apparent multiplicity of sources in her voice
Whose murmur could be heard,
When far from her, even on another continent.

Her presence both concrete
And forever vaporous.

She was never closer to him
Than when she was away .

While he would already start horribly missing her
As soon as she nestled against his shoulder.

He knew...
... He knew that she would inevitably become nothing more

Than burns from cooled radiations
On the retina of memory.

Until only...
... Impressions, forms...

... Would appear
On the humid other side of a tearful diaphragm.

Such was the devastation of the landscape
That he caught himself renouncing for the first time...

... Sight: The sense that all by itself

Had totally... absolutely defined him.

Sight... Which in a world without her
Had lost its purpose.

Reflections on the film At First Sight *with Val Kilmer where a man regains his sight only to lose it.*

PETIT À PETIT [LITTLE BY LITTLE]

Il y avait toujours eu quelque chose d'irréel dans les détails :
Les instants semblaient trop souvent hors du possible.

Les lois de l'univers et du bonheur
Joyeusement détournées, transgressées :

Le regard trop éternel.
La peau trop soyeuse.

Sa voix aux sources apparemment multiples
Dont le murmure s'entendait, loin d'elle, sur un autre
continent.

Sa présence à la fois concrète
Et à jamais vaporeuse.

Elle n'était jamais tant à ses côtés
Que lorsqu'elle en était absente.

Alors qu'elle commençait déjà à lui manquer horriblement
Dès qu'elle se trouvait contre son épaule.

Il savait...
... Il savait qu'elle deviendrait inévitablement

Brûlures de radiations refroidies
Sur la rétine de la mémoire.

Jusqu'à ce que seules
Des impressions, des formes

Ne se laissent distinguer
De l'autre côté humide d'un diaphragme larmoyant.

La dévastation du paysage étant telle
Qu'il se prit à renier pour la première fois...

... La vue : Le sens qui à lui seul

L'avait totalement... absolument défini.

La vue...Qui dans un monde en son absence
Avait perdu sa raison d'être.

Réflexions sur le film Premier regard *avec Val Kilmer où un homme recouvre la vue et la reperd.*

A WAY WITH WORDS

Stylish clothes and European manners.
Smart remarks and explosive sarcasm.

Unexpected hyperbolas
Cleverly hidden understatements.

Impeccable résumé and factual recall
For executive meetings and Friday nights trivia.

For her... Class in classy short black skirts.
Italian cuts of suits and paper thin leather shoes for him.

Like Samurai warriors wielding sharp blades,
Lightening quick reflexes fending off verbal blows.

Intellectual skirmishes across the lunch table
Turning into a foreplay of events
Of volcanic energy bubbling from visceral heat.

Unblinking glances trying to possess with eyes
What yet, cannot be had by the embrace.

Artifice of the artificial... of purported jaded attitude
To hide under sheets of posturing
What will be revealed under the sheets of lubricity.

Their respective lives had reached the point
Of easily defining themselves
Simply by what they already contained.

Opposites in so many ways...
      ... That they inevitably had to meet each other...
On the opposite side of their worlds:

Seemingly soul mates by fulfilling in the other
The waiting gapping cavity of the other soul's resting place.

They both had evolved up that evolutionary tree

Of the Happy Few…

Living in that proverbial corner office
With city skyline at their feet
And waiting reservations at favorite French restaurant.

Endowed both with questioning minds.
Both well known for their sense of humor:

"Seems like a nice kid" as throw away line.

Similar to the giant Titans of old, they absorbed life
And thus received strength from their social surroundings.

Like all powerful authentic tragedies
They were at their apogee
When they came in each other's lives.

The symbols of moral challenges
Have changed little since classical times.

No need for mythological representations:
The mechanism for unbridled passion is still the same.

Shakespeare and Racine did not invent anything,
Nor end it by the teaching power of their analysis.

They just knew better than most
Where the strings are located…

This man and this woman should have known,
By the changing appearance, in their own minds,
Of the Formica and stainless steel furniture of the gloomy cafeteria

Turning into a Moroccan setting of soft pillows and scented oils:
With all the fiery trappings of an Oriental Delacroix painting.

Inspired by the theatre of office dynamics.

FRAGILE EMBRACE

He had thought, beforehand,
That it would be the glance...
    ... the virility of the voice...
    ... the sincerity of feelings...

That would reemerge in his soul.

He was hoping for a familiar remark...
    ... a known head movement...
    ... a particular parting of the lips...
    ... that gentle touch of her shoulder against his.

Any and all of these quasi vaporous memories of her
Should have been enough to re hydrate the crystals of their past.

It was... instead, his astonishment
Of how close to the surface she had carnally remained in his soul:

For it was when he again held her in his arms to kiss her,
That his body was overwhelmed by the natural...
    ... The uncontrollable natural ease...

Of the reconstruction... of hers...
Upon sensing the memory of the fragility of her flesh.

The months... the solidity of years of separation
Had been no match against the fluidity of her presence.

Inspired by another Nineteenth Century novel.

A FEW MORE STEPS

He couldn't help it...
Emotional metaphors and clichés
Were overwhelming his heart.

The early New England Spring Sun, at its feeble best,
Was trying to warm the street
As well as their paces toward 'their breakfast place.'

A place of refuge and remembrance from and of Time for both.
An immersion in the remaining puddles of their past hours:
But the ambient chill let them know that things were not the same.

Gone now was the symbiotic walk of old.
Gone the unconscious need to feel the other
Through the layers of clothing as they avoided the uneven stones.

Gone the instinctive glance upon one another
In rhythm with the need to look down at the side walk.

Gone also the natural authenticity of words
Whispered by wanting lips in the Labradorean cold.

There was a funeral essence
To this attempt at a walk into their past.

This street where the very warmth of their presence
Had previously rendered the glacial surroundings unimportant.

That is when they reached that telephone poll:
Inanimate presence of the silent Universe
That would force upon them non verbalized truths.

He had expected that it would force her to come closer to his side:
    ... She always had done so...

Instead she swerved into the street...
    ... And away from his waiting shoulder...

Thus, before and after that telephone poll
Was the same woman:

Respectful of their past and of his feelings,
Generous in a classical way... a true lady.
Distinguished in disguising the inevitable.

And so, before and after that slight but symbolic detour
Around the telephone poll,
He could still maintain his emotional honor,

Having been spared humiliation:
He still had his integrity of the illusionary...

    ... But not much else was left from the wealth of their past.

Inspired by a viewing of the old classics A Summer Place, Splendor in the Grass, *and the irretrievability of Time and Love.*

NO NEED TO KNOW

All these inquisitive looks… from his into hers,
Where he had recognized evidence
Of the shade of another presence.

Having been allowed
Into some of her well defined partitions,

He had been privileged
To have known instants of tempting voyeurism.

There seemed to exist, in her fertile world,
A natural authenticity of Things:
The uncoiling of primordial energy.

He had wandered… wide eyed… in that proverbial oasis
And tasted the sugary dark brown dates…

… The ones from the highest hidden timid reaches.

Drunk the tepid oasis water
That reinforced the warm corruption of gratification.

Like late Summer afternoon bumblebees,
Full of the pollen of life made of raspy yellow hues,

He had touched pleasure,
But had never… never been allowed…
To enter that other space of her being:

The one that quieted his thoughts
When his thoughts turned to her.

The one that hid behind a non sequitur
When an implicit question was explicitly ignored.

That space that left him believing
That a piece of her life had been carefully sealed
Behind enormous boulders of rich complicated emotions.

If Only...

Not unlike these harem beauties buried alive
In order to protect some uncontrolled royal eccentricity.

He had never asked... and was never told:
_ "I had no need to know" he thought to himself
Drowned by the lyrics...

"Some Things Are Better Left Unsaid" by Hall and Oates

IF ONLY...

The inlet and its next generation of ducks: still there.
The dunes with different footprints: but the same warmth.

The coffee table: different napkins under its leg but still wobbling.
The ride from the airport, just as congested: not as joyful.

Concerts: with one reservation. Italian take out: for one.
He had adjusted to his emotional juxtaposition on things.

His envies could still be seen,
But only through a transparent film:
A reminder of the new protocol imposed on his heart.

These envies and their solidity in Space and Time
Having learned to silently coexist in the world.

It was only when essences of Proustian ghosts would appear
That the past would regenerate in the humidity of memories.

Sprouts of shy greenish buttons of hope would appear,
But then would soon dry in the absence of encouragement:
And he would readapt to the barren landscape.

This, and all sorts of other images came to his mind:
Knowing that, in a post Santa Claus world,

He would have to learn to live and get along:
Like Sisyphus of old meaninglessly pushing his bolder.

He would learn, nevertheless, to admire
The darkest of darkest of coals
That would, from time to time, soil his hands.

And so, in the manner of tragedies, great and small,
Only center stage hopeful activity would drive the days,

With a few interludes of touching moments
Found in the magic happiness of metaphors of childhood:

If Only...

Exemplified by the tender presence of one's favorite truck.

———————————————

He felt no anger in his heart. No bitterness:
Having wandered into enough sweetness to last a lifetime.

"If only..." he however murmured wistfully
In the mournful sound of the seagulls.

He could merely hope, that a generous god
Would see to it, that he would die first;

And thus be granted the lesser of the pains:
That of not living and not knowing a world without her.

The reader can chose a favorite Nineteenth Century Novel as a template for the above.

GLOSSARY OF WORDS AND TERMS

This glossary of words, names and terms is added for the convenience of readers to enhance their enjoyment of and access to the full range of language and meaning used in the poems. Many of Jean-Yves Solinga's poems are translations from French and are littered with words of particular cultural and literary reference from this language. There are also religious and historical references and other terms which may be unfamiliar to some readers. The briefest definition or explanation is provided only to support the meaning in the poem.

Apogee: The farthest or highest point; the apex.

Baudelaire, Charles: Nineteenth Century French poet whose *La chevelure* is one the great example of *Prose Lyrique or Poèmes en prose*.

Beatitudes: Supreme blessedness; exalted happiness.

Beckett, Samuel: (13 April 1906 – 22 December 1989) was an Irish avant-garde writer, dramatist and poet, writing in English and French. Of interest, in particular, here is the play *Waiting for Godot* in which the characters wait for an ever absent Godot.

Camus, Albert: An agnostic writer and moralist of the Absurd. A philosophy where man confronts his consciousness of the meaninglessness of life. Best known for The Stranger whose main character exemplifies the consciousness of the Absurd. Camus is part of a long line of moralists who try to deal with good and evil in their vision of a godless universe.

Canyon du Verdon: Majestic canyon of Upper Provence, France.

Château-Neuf-du-Pape: Hearty Red Wine of Provence.

Dante: Of interest in particular here is the image of the ideal woman in the figure of Beatrice.

Danziger Bridge: Bridge on Lake Pontchartrain in New Orleans.

Deus ex machina: (Latin for "god from the machine) Is a plot device whereby a seemingly inextricable problem is suddenly and abruptly solved with the contrived and unexpected intervention of some new character, ability, or object. The term now denotes something that appears suddenly and unexpectedly and provides an artificial solution to an apparently insoluble difficulty. Originally it was a stage device in Greek and Roman drama in which a god appeared in the sky by means of a crane (Greek, mechane) to resolve the plot of a play.

Delacroix, Eugène: (26 April 1798 – 13 August 1863) was a French Romantic artist regarded from the outset of his career as the leader of the French Romantic school

Divine Comedy: see Dante.

Euclidean: For over two thousand years, this adjective was unnecessary because no other sort of geometry had been conceived. Euclid's axioms seemed so intuitively obvious that any theorem proved from them was deemed true in an absolute sense. Today, however, many other self-consistent non-Euclidean geometries are known, the first ones having been discovered in the early 19th century. An implication of Einstein's theory of general relativity is that Euclidean space is a good approximation to the properties of physical space only where the gravitational field is not too strong

Expurgatory: Act of removing.

Faites vos jeux... rien ne va plus: Place your bets... no more bets.

Gide, André Paul Guillaume: (22 November 1869 – 19 February 1951) was a French author and winner of the Nobel Prize in literature in 1947. Known for his lyrical passages describing his sense of freedom and availability to new found sensuality.

Godot: Is an absent character in the play, *Waiting for Godot* by Samuel Becket.

Inexistent: Having no existence; nonexistent.

Labradorean cold: The part of the province of Newfoundland and Labrador, Canada, on the North American mainland. Its coastline was visited by Norse seamen as early as the tenth century. The area later became a possession of the Hudson's Bay Company and was claimed by Quebec until 1927, when it was awarded to Newfoundland.

Machina: see Deus ex machina.

Mallarmé, Stéphane: Symbolist French poet of the end of the Nineteenth Century.

Mana, Laura: Whose movie *Sexo por Compassion* gives a splendid analysis of humanity.

Maquisards: French World War Two Underground.

Melon de Cavaillon: Aromatic melons of Provence.

Mons: Village in the hills of Provence, France.

Montagne [Mont] Sainte-Victoire: Mount near Aix-en-Provence painted repeatedly by Paul Cézanne.

Musset [de Mussett-Pathay], Alfred Louis Charles: (11 December 1810 – 2 May 1857) was a French dramatist, poet, and novelist. Along with his poetry, he is known for writing *La Confession d'un enfant du siècle* (The Confession of a Child of the Century, autobiographical) from 1836. His passionate and heartbreaking relationship with George Sand [a woman writer Aurore Dupin] gave rise to some of the most beautiful romantic era poems.

Pétanque: (also known as Boules.) A popular game of French Botchie played with metal spheres in any square of Provençal village. Usually followed by a celebratory round at the corner Café.

Pinède: French for pine forest.

Pontchartrain Lake: A salt water lake (actually not a lake but an estuary connected to the Gulf of Mexico) directly north of New Orleans. Lake Pontchartrain is named after Louis Phélypeaux, comte de Pontchartrain, the French Minister of the Marine, Chancellor of France and Controller-General of Finances during the reign of France's "Sun King," Louis XIV, for whom Louisiana is named.

Proust, Marcel: Early Twentieth Century French writer of *À la recherche du temps perdu [Remembrance of Things Past]* in which he analyzes how the senses bring back the past.

Racine, Jean: (December 1639 – April 21, 1699) was a French dramatist, of Classical Tragedies, one of the "Big Three" of 17th century France (along with Molière and Corneille), and one of the most important literary figures in the Western tradition.

Sisyphus: Character of Greek Mythology punished by the gods and forced to endlessly push a bolder up a hill.

Souk: Moroccan market.

Vaison la romaine: Roman ruins in Provence.

INDEX OF TITLES AND FIRST LINES

Poem titles are in bold, and the first lines are in regular text with page numbers on the right.

A

A Beautiful Mind	39
A Blindness of the Soul	62
A Farmer in Kansas	47
A Few More Steps	98
All in a Steamer Trunk	38
All these hours, all this coffee… in his favorite space	55
All these inquisitive looks… from his into hers,	100
Arrogance	6
A sort of unease sets in after three days:	5
A uniform of electric blue,	43
A Way With Words	95

B

Behind the Curtain	24
Between Literature and Reality	73

C

Can't Take It With You	71
Compassionate Sex	68

D

Death Watch	78
Des années trop tard	64
Digitized Happiness	60
Dream Sequence 1	40
Dream Sequence 2	42

E

Elle existe là, où les muses finissent leur vie:	58
Elvis in Provence	20
Emanations	83
Émanations	85
Entre la littérature et la réalité	74

F

First Time	87
For a while… They were united in gentle splendor :	7
Fragile Embrace	97

G

Gated People	31
Grande Illusion	22
Greater than life… he stood there.	20

H

He could not reconcile the mournful ambiance	78
He couldn't help it…	98
He had heard about her.	73
He had lived in the land of plenty…	81
He had met her	22
He had thought, beforehand,	97
He had thought that she had come over for him.	68
"Help the People… Help them!"	28
He seems to disappear	45
He stood there, his heart and soul	24
He was back in the Medina of that little village,	48
His steps seemed to remember…	77

I

Icons of contradictions whirled in their minds:	87
If Only…	102

Il y avait toujours eu quelque chose d'irréel dans les détails :	93
Il avait entendu parler d'elle.	74
In his heart where reigned	47
In some future time in our digitized destiny,	50
Intouchable	58
It is there that she exists. There where Muses' lives end:	56
It happened on a walk	9

L

Landscapes	55
Le Souk à Salé	27
Life, mindlessly multiplying life and demeaning it.	19
Like a last supper... but for just a few select guests.	31
Little by Little	91
Little Voices of Guilt and Joy	89

M

Man on a Wire	7
Men in Cages	19
Mesh Mãsh	48
Molecular Memory	77
Much too often, cultures,	26

N

No Need To Know	100
Nothing like a bath in the cross currents of confusion...	34

O

Of Beautiful Uniforms and Ugliness	43
Of Cats	5
Of Existentialism and DNA	32
Of Macro and Micro Thought	36
Of Microchips Wafers and Flake of Humanism	34
Of Stardust and Morality	16
Only biblical analogies came to his mind.	63

Outside of the Temple   2

P

Parfums aux noms sophistiqués d'avenues parisiennes   85
Perfumes with brands of sophisticated Parisian avenues,   83
Petit à petit [Little by Little]   93
Proustian Scene   69

R

Reflection   75
Rien que des analogies bibliques lui venaient à l'esprit.   64
Ripples of fresh water from dark green inner hills   42
Running on empty… in empty street.   60

S

Scalloped sided black and white picture.   39
Scan # 916   50
She had prided herself in self awareness.   62
She was at the limit of perfection   75
Somewhere, someone had these remains of them.   38
Sparkling intelligence and stellar accomplishments.   15
Stylish clothes and European manners.   95

T

The Danziger Bridge   28
The Fable of the Artist and his Muse   81
The End of the World   13
The inlet and its next generation of ducks: still there.   102
The Magic Field   9
The Pyramid Builder   45
There always had been something unreal in the details: 91
There had always been   69
The Souk in Salé   26
They had done it.   40
They were prisoners of their choices.   89

Time and people had divided themselves.	65
To the East, the hills that open up on Cannes.	13
Trop souvent les cultures,	27
Truly heartfelt sadness.	36

U

Ultimate and pitiful. Sterile arrogance.	6
Untouchable	56

W

Waiting for Happiness to Come Back	65
What to do:	32
Wise words,	71
With the respectful steps of a High Priest,	2

Y

Years Too Late	63

www.ingramcontent.com/pod-product-compliance
Lightning Source LLC
Chambersburg PA
CBHW080515110426
42742CB00017B/3119